Betsy Ross

Patriot of
Philadelphia

Betsy Ross

Patriot

of Philadelphia

JUDITH ST. GEORGE

ILLUSTRATIONS BY

SASHA MERET

HENRY HOLT AND COMPANY
NEW YORK

Thanks to Frances K. Delmar, historian, past program director for
Landmarks' Elderhostel, and museum consultant, for reading the manuscript.

Henry Holt and Company, LLC
Publishers since 1866
175 Fifth Avenue
New York, New York 10010
www.henryholtchildrensbooks.com

Henry Holt® is a registered
trademark of Henry Holt and Company, LLC.

Library of Congress Cataloging-in-Publication Data
St. George, Judith.
Betsy Ross: patriot of Philadelphia / by Judith St. George.
p.   cm.
Includes bibliographical references and index.
Summary: The personal struggles of the woman generally credited with having created
the first American flag are set against the backdrop of the colonists' fight for independence.
1. Ross, Betsy, 1752–1836—Juvenile literature.   2. Revolutionaries—United States—Biography—
Juvenile literature.   3. United States—History—Revolution, 1775–1783—Biography—Juvenile
literature.   4. Flags—United States—History—18th century—Juvenile literature.   5. Philadelphia
(Pa.)—Biography—Juvenile literature.   [1. Ross, Betsy, 1752–1836.   2. Revolutionaries.
3. United States—History—Revolution, 1775–1783.   4. Flags—United States.]   I. Title.
E302.6.R77S7   1997   973.3'092   [B]—DC21   97-9734

ISBN-13: 978-0-8050-5439-2 / ISBN-10: 0-8050-5439-1
First Edition—1997
Printed in the United States of America on acid-free paper. ∞
7   9   11   13   15   14   12   10   8

To my Philadelphia friend, Liz

Betsy Ross
Patriot of
Philadelphia

CHAPTER 1

Like most Quaker children in Philadelphia, Betsy Griscom went to the Friends Public School. Six mornings a week, she got up early, helped with chores, and then went to school. She wore a plain gray dress, a clean white apron, and a white cap. For eight hours, she sat on a hard wooden bench, memorizing, reciting, and writing in her hornbook. It wasn't much fun and Schoolmaster was strict. On Saturdays, he took a birch twig and switched those boys and girls who hadn't behaved or done their lessons during the week.

School wasn't all work. There was time during the day to do what Betsy loved best: stitching her sampler, working on her quilt, or making baby clothes for her family's newest baby. She had always had a talent for sewing and whenever she had a spare moment, she grabbed her needle and thread.

Betsy's parents, Samuel and Rebecca, were Quakers. The Griscoms attended Meeting on First Day, or Sunday, and Fifth Day, or Thursday. They practiced their religion by saying daily prayers, helping their neighbors, and working hard. Their home, furniture, clothes, and speech were plain.

The Griscom children weren't allowed to play music, dance, go to the theater, read fiction, or play cards. But Philadelphia was the largest city in the American colonies, and there was plenty to do. Betsy and her sisters and brother enjoyed going on picnics. They also had hayride and sailing parties. In the winter they sledded, skated, and went sleigh riding.

Elizabeth Griscom, always known as Betsy, was born in 1752 on a farm in West Jersey. Two years later, the Griscoms moved to Philadelphia, where Betsy started school. At age twelve, Betsy's school days were over. Someday she would be a wife and mother, and school was no longer considered necessary.

Being finished with school meant Betsy had many chores to do at home: cooking, cleaning, spinning, marketing, washing, ironing, mending, and sewing.

She and her father's aunt, Great Aunt Sarah, did most of the mending and sewing.

Betsy and Great Aunt Sarah had always been drawn to one another, perhaps because they were so much alike. They were gifted at needlework, and they were also strong-minded, independent thinkers.

Great Aunt Sarah, who was in her seventies, lived with Betsy's family. Years before, she had started her own business when businesses were run only by men. She had made and sold corsets and undergarments. She also sold hard cider to taverns and inns. She didn't put up with any nonsense, either. If a customer didn't pay a bill, she published that person's name in the newspaper. Aunt Deborah and Cousin Rebecca lived with the Griscoms, too. All three women helped Betsy's mother with the children and housework.

In 1764, the year that Betsy finished school, her

family moved again. Her father, Samuel, had a successful construction business and he had built a large brick house on Arch Street. Betsy was delighted. At last there would be enough room for everyone. Betsy couldn't ever remember a time when her mother hadn't just had a baby or wasn't pregnant with the next one. She gave birth to seventeen children in all.

Soon after they moved, Samuel announced that Betsy was old enough to learn a trade. He decided that the upholstery business was best suited to her needlework talents. That was fine with Betsy. She was becoming an attractive young woman with thick chestnut hair, a fair complexion, and beautiful blue eyes. She may have been slender and delicate, but she was full of energy and eager to go on to something new.

CHAPTER 2

John Webster's Upholstery Shop was well known in Philadelphia. Like the Griscoms, John Webster was a Quaker. When Samuel spoke to him about taking Betsy on as an apprentice, he agreed at once. Friend Webster remembered Betsy. She had come into his shop on an errand one day and noticed a seamstress struggling with her piecework. Betsy had stepped right up and said that she knew how to do the work the way it should he done. And she did. As an apprentice, Betsy wouldn't be paid. She would continue living with her family but would work in the shop during the day.

Betsy started her apprenticeship with her usual enthusiasm. To her surprise, she discovered there was more to the business than just making slipcovers and upholstering furniture. The shop workers also hung wallpaper, fitted ships' cabins, covered umbrellas, and stuffed mattresses. They made venetian blinds, bed hangings, draperies, tablecloths, carpets, blankets, flags, tents, and more.

At first Betsy was given the most boring tasks. While everyone else was cutting, basting, and sewing, she was bringing supplies up from the cellar and stocking them on shelves. She also swept the shop, ironed fabric, and ran errands. It was terribly frustrating. Betsy knew that she could do the needlework as well, if not better, than anyone else. Her stitches were finer. She could work more quickly. She even had a better eye for design and color.

At last, John Webster began to appreciate Betsy's talents. Little by little, he gave her more to do. First she was allowed to lay out patterns on the fabric. Then she could cut the fabric and prepare the pieces for sewing. Next she basted and finally she stitched. One fine day, she made a pair of curtains from beginning to end. Although she still wasn't being paid, she took pride in her work.

Betsy's hours were even longer than her school days had been. But tired as she was when she got home, she enjoyed telling Great Aunt Sarah what went on during the day. She described the beautiful brocades and silks that had just arrived by ship from England. They both must have laughed as she told about the wealthy customer whose lap dog was attacked by the Websters' cat. Then there was the story of the worker who uphol- stered a chair with the fabric wrong-side out. What shone through all of Betsy's tales was the pleasure that she took in what she was doing.

Betsy looked forward to those happy times with Great Aunt Sarah. She had learned everything she knew about needlework from her aunt. Like Great Aunt Sarah, someday Betsy would have her very own shop.

CHAPTER 3

B etsy made new friends at Webster's. She especially liked John Ross, another young apprentice. Tall and dark, John was also easy to talk to. He and Betsy had a lot in common. They had both experienced the death of brothers and sisters. Betsy had lost six younger siblings, Samuel, Martha, Ann, Samuel II, and twins Joseph and Abigail. She had fed them, changed them, and delighted in their first smiles and words. She had loved them and would miss them forever. Of John's five brothers and sisters, only his sister, Johanna, was still living.

Betsy and John had something else in common. They both wanted to open their own upholstery shop. John had grown up in New Castle, Delaware. He was the son of an Anglican minister, the Reverend Aeneas Ross. His family had struggled to make ends meet on a clergyman's salary and most of John's clothes had been hand-me-downs from church members. Because John made up his mind that he wouldn't be poor, he had left home and come to Philadelphia.

There was another coincidence. Betsy and John had both been born in 1752. But Betsy's birth date was special. It was January 1, 1752. Although March 25 had been the first day of the new year for centuries, in 1752, January 1 became New Year's Day. Betsy's birthday fell on the first day of the first month of the first year of the new calendar.

Over time, Betsy and John's friendship changed, grew, and became something more. They fell in love. It wasn't long before Betsy's parents found out about John Ross and what he meant to their daughter. As far as Samuel and Rebecca Griscom were concerned, Betsy couldn't have made a worse choice. She had chosen a young man who wasn't a Quaker.

For years there had been bad feelings between Philadelphia's Quakers, who were members of the Religious Society of Friends, and Anglicans, who were members of the Church of England. When the Quakers arrived to settle Philadelphia in the 1600s, they treated American Indians fairly. During the French and Indian War that began in 1754, the Quakers resigned their seats in the Pennsylvania Assembly. Their faith forbid them to bear arms or support warfare in any way. The Anglicans and Presbyterians, who took over the Assembly, resented the Quakers' stand on nonviolence. They were also angry at the Quakers for refusing to pay taxes to defend Philadelphia against Indian attacks.

If Betsy married John, there was a good chance she would be asked to leave the Society of Friends. Their Book of Discipline read: "Mixing in Marriage with Those not of our Professions is an unequal Yoking which brings ill Consequences to the Parties as well as Grief to their honest Friends and Relatives and frequently ends in Woe and Ruin of Themselves and their Children."

Neither Samuel and Rebecca's disapproval nor the bad feelings between Quakers and Anglicans mattered to Betsy and John. They were in love and planned to get married. Betsy's parents advised, urged, and begged their daughter to reconsider, but Betsy wouldn't be swayed. Furthermore, she made it clear that when John had his own upholstery shop, she would work for him.

Finally, that big day came. John opened for business in the house he leased on Chestnut Street. The *Pennsylvania Gazette* on February 24, 1773, announced, "JOHN ROSS TAKES this Method to inform the PUBLIC, That he has opened an UPHOLDER's SHOP, in Chestnut-street, between Front and Second-streets, where all Kinds of Upholder's Business is done, in the neatest and most fashionable Manner, on the shortest Notice, with Care and Dispatch."

With the opening of the shop, the time had come for Betsy and John to marry. Although Betsy's parents still wouldn't consent, Betsy and John were both twenty-one. They would take matters into their own hands.

Cetsy and John's talk of marriage was cut short by the death of eighty-year-old Great Aunt Sarah. She had been in failing health for some time, but Betsy took her aunt's death hard. Great Aunt Sarah had sat beside her hour after hour teaching, correcting, and making her rip out her stitches and start again. And she had taught Betsy something very important, to stand on her own two feet.

Betsy had never let Great Aunt Sarah down when she was alive, and she wouldn't let Great Aunt Sarah down now. She would be faithful to her feelings and marry John, despite her parents' disapproval.

With John working from dawn to dusk in his new shop, Betsy made all the arrangements. A family wedding was out of the question. They would have to elope and tell the Griscoms later. Several of Betsy's Quaker friends had slipped over to New Jersey and been married by a justice of the peace. That was what she and John would do.

Right away they ran into trouble. If they wanted to be married in New Jersey without permission from Betsy's parents, they would have to post five hundred pounds for a marriage bond. The bond guaranteed that they were both twenty-one and there was no legal reason why they shouldn't be married.

Five hundred pounds! That was a good deal more money than most people made in a year. Betsy certainly didn't have that kind of money and neither did John. He had been putting everything he earned back into his shop. Finally Betsy came up with a solution. The Griscoms had been friends with the Hugg family in New Jersey going back two generations. From years of visiting back and forth with her New Jersey relatives, Betsy knew the Huggs well. Maybe William Hugg, Jr., would be willing to help.

William had inherited a tavern from his father and made a good living. When Betsy spoke to him, he agreed to sign for the bond. That was it. Betsy and John set the date, November 4, 1773.

Betsy managed the other details, too. Taking the ferry across the Delaware River to New Jersey was risky. Someone might see them. Instead, Betsy asked her older sister, Sarah, and her seaman husband, Captain William Donaldson, to row them across.

Because November 4 fell on a workday, the wedding party couldn't leave until after dark. It was a long row in the open skiff. A damp wind kicked up white caps that splashed everyone on board with a freezing spray.

After landing on the Jersey shore, William hid his skiff in a tangle of shrubs. The four of them then headed out on foot for Gloucestertown and Hugg's Tavern.

Young William Hugg had done his job well. Justice of the Peace James Bowman was waiting. The marriage license had been filled out. A cheerful fire burned in the tavern's fireplace. With the Donaldsons and William Hugg as witnesses, Justice Bowman began. The roaring fire crackled, while a grandfather clock ticked off the time. A few minutes later, Betsy and John had become husband and wife.

CHAPTER 5

After the wedding, Betsy moved into John's house. Although she helped out in the front-room shop, work was slow coming in. It was just one of many upholstery shops in Philadelphia and most of the others had been in business a long time.

While the newlyweds were trying to get started, Philadelphia was in an uproar over the tea tax. The colonists had to pay a tax to Great Britain on all British East India Company tea. Most Americans resented the tax and bought or smuggled in their tea from other countries. The British objected. In 1773, the British parliament decided that only East India Company tea could be sold in the American colonies.

Americans everywhere were furious. They wanted

to buy tea from whomever they pleased. Because the British didn't allow the colonists to vote in Parliament, the tea tax was a tax over which Americans had no say. A cry went up. Boycott British tea!

Philadelphians soon learned that two Quaker business partners, Abel James and Henry Drinker, planned to bring the British ship *Polly* into Philadelphia. The *Polly* carried a cargo of East India Company tea. Because the two men were Quakers, everyone knew that they wouldn't oppose British authority in any way. Most Philadelphians felt differently.

Meetings were held all over town. First, James and Drinker were ordered to stop the delivery. Then a warning was sent to Captain Ayres, the master of the *Polly*, that was signed by the Committee for Tarring and Feathering and dated November 27, 1773. "What think you, Captain, of a Halter around your Neck . . . ten Gallons of liquid Tar . . . with the Feathers of a dozen Geese laid over that to enliven your appearance!"

Abel James and Henry Drinker put up a bold front and continued business as usual. Captain Ayres didn't take the threat seriously either. He anchored the *Polly* on the New Jersey side of the Delaware River and arrived in Philadelphia by pilot boat. His bravado didn't last long. When he heard about the thousands of angry

Americans who had gathered in the State House Yard, he quickly returned to the *Polly*. He set sail without unloading so much as a single chest of tea.

Although Abel James was Betsy's uncle, Betsy and John agreed with the rebels. They may not have been among the hotheads who gathered in the State House Yard, but they both opposed the tea tax.

Soon after the tea tax uprising, Betsy and John were faced with another problem. This one was closer to home. As Betsy had expected, her fellow Quakers objected to her marriage. By marrying outside her faith, she had been disobedient. In April 1774 a committee of women Friends arrived at the Ross's Chestnut Street home to urge Betsy to repent.

Betsy was friendly but firm. She was not going to change her mind. The committee reported back to the elders that Betsy "did not appear inclined to repent or condemn her breach of duty."

Word spread quickly that a special meeting had been called in which Betsy would be asked to leave the Religious Society of Friends. It was called a "disownment" proceeding. Despite the gossip, Betsy continued to welcome customers to the shop. She went to market and drew water from the nearby public well with a pleasant word and a smile for her neighbors.

Betsy was next told that she would be allowed to make a statement at her disownment proceedings. But she had nothing more to say. And so the proceedings went on without her. The leader of the men's meeting was Uncle Abel James's partner, Henry Drinker. The women's meeting was run by Hannah Cathrall, who had taught Betsy her ABCs at Rebecca Jones' School years before.

The Religious Society of Friends recorded Betsy's disownment in their minutes with such phrases as ". . . married to a man of another religious persuasion—without the consent of her parents . . . disorderly and undutiful conduct . . . she hath disunited herself from the Religious Fellowship with us."

A few weeks later, a committee again arrived at the Rosses'. The Quakers were willing to give Betsy another chance to repent. Although Betsy found it harder to be friendly this time, she politely refused. At the June 1774 Meeting, the committee declared that Betsy "appeared to be satisfied with Friends' proceedings in her case."

After seven months of gossip, talk, committee visits, and calls to repent, the subject was at last closed. Betsy was no longer a member of the Religious Society of Friends. Finally, she and John could get on with their lives.

CHAPTER 6

Betsy and John's business didn't improve. The disownment proceedings had taken a lot of their time and energy. Perhaps if they moved, trade would pick up. They decided to lease larger quarters in a section of town where there were other upholstery and craftsmen shops.

Leaving their little Chestnut Street house, they moved to a two-and-a-half story brick house on Arch Street between Second and Third Streets. It was only a block or so from where Betsy had grown up. And the neighborhood of small shops was just what they wanted. To advertise their business, they placed a handsomely upholstered chair in their front window, where passersby were sure to see it.

During his years at Webster's, John had acquired a
full set of tools. He owned a mallet, pincers, strapping
pliers, shears, tack lifter, upholsterer's hammer, screw
wrench, scrapers, chisel, punch, webbing stretcher,
awl, and a knife.

Betsy was ready for business, too, with threads,
thimbles, beeswax, smoothing iron, and a forty-five-
inch ell-rule for measuring cloth. As the mark of her
trade, she attached a silver hook to her dress that held
a pair of scissors and a silver-ringed needle ball on
two silver chains. It was called a chatelaine. She was
always careful not to lose any pins or needles. They
were handmade and very expensive. A single pin
sometimes cost as much as sixpence. Betsy had never
forgotten the jingle that Great Aunt Sarah had taught
her.

See a pin and let it lie;
You'll want that pin before you die.
See a pin and pick it up
And you'll always have good luck.

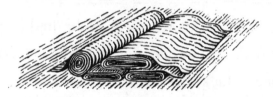

Unfortunately, business continued to be slow. Betsy and John had spent a lot of money to make the move and stock up on fabric and supplies. They needed every customer they could get.

On Sundays, they put the shop behind them and attended Christ Church. Betsy may have been used to hearing the lovely peal of the Christ Church bells, but she wasn't used to Church of England ways. Instead of simple Quaker dress, Anglican women paraded to church in silks and brocades. The men wore velvet breeches, ruffled shirts, and powdered wigs.

Betsy was even more puzzled by Church of England

services. Instead of silence, there was organ music. The people joined in the hymn singing, prayers, and psalms while standing, sitting, or kneeling. Betsy found herself standing while everyone else was sitting, and sitting while everyone else was kneeling. There were certainly no periods of quiet as everyone waited for the Inner Light to prompt a member to speak. Instead, the minister preached such long sermons that Betsy had to pinch herself to stay awake.

If Sunday services were bewildering, Sunday afternoons were delightful. Betsy and John went walking, called on friends, or as a special treat, hired a carriage for a ride into the countryside.

But all around them, unrest was growing. The tea tax had stirred up the people, and the British were losing patience with their American colonies.

In the spring of 1774, Paul Revere rode into Philadelphia. He had traveled from Boston to New York, and from New York to Philadelphia. The British, he reported, were about to close down the Port of Boston.

He also arrived with a summons. Representatives from all thirteen colonies were to meet in a Continental Congress to discuss the burning issues of the day. The date was set for September 1774, and the location was set, too. As the largest and most central city in America, Philadelphia would be the meeting place. Like it or not, Philadelphia was about to become the capital of American resistance. Betsy and John's lives would never be the same.

CHAPTER 7

Betsy and John's days were spent from dawn to dusk in their shop. Each week seemed to bring in more customers. As their business grew, their front room filled with furniture being repaired, stripped, refinished, covered, and upholstered. Bolts of fabric, rolls of piping, tape and braid, boxes of iron tacks, upholstery pins, and brass nails, canvas webbing, tassels, and fringes filled the shelves.

Meanwhile, tensions rose in Philadelphia as plans went ahead for the Continental Congress. American Patriots handed out pamphlets that attacked British rule. Wealthy Loyalist merchants and importers made it clear they supported the king. Refusing to challenge

authority or even take a stand, Quakers angered Patriots and Loyalists alike.

The Continental Congress met for the first time in Carpenters' Hall on September 5, 1774, near Betsy and John's shop. Delegates had arrived from New Hampshire, Massachusetts, Rhode Island, Connecticut, New York, New Jersey, Pennsylvania, Delaware, Maryland, Virginia, North Carolina, and South Carolina. Only Georgia wasn't represented. Patrick Henry, a lawyer from Virginia, made a fiery speech on the very first day. "The distinctions between Virginians, Pennsylvanians, New Yorkers, New Englanders are no more. I am not a Virginian but an American," he declared.

Before the delegates adjourned six weeks later, they sent a formal list of complaints to the king. They called for a halt to all British imports. They also proposed that colonial militia units be formed.

John Ross was deeply affected by what the Continental Congress had accomplished. He decided to enlist in the local Citizens Guard. The Citizens Guard was organized to protect Philadelphia's citizens in time of danger. Its members also guarded military stores that had been secretly stockpiled around the city. John was assigned guard duty along the wharves.

Luckily, he made his rounds at night, which left him free to work in the shop during the day.

The winter passed quickly, with both Betsy and John keeping busy, especially John, who continued his Citizen Guard duty. With no more fabrics coming in from Great Britain, Betsy spent her time patching and darning slipcovers, draperies, and bedcurtains. She also mended both ladies' and men's clothing.

As spring was beginning to green up Philadelphia, a Boston post rider arrived at City Tavern. He reported that two battles had taken place in Massachusetts on April 19 and 20, 1775. British troops had clashed at Lexington and Concord with local farmers called Minutemen. Like everyone else, Betsy and John were caught by surprise. It now seemed certain that the colonies were headed for war.

A Second Continental Congress had already been called. Delegates from all thirteen colonies, including Georgia, arrived in Philadelphia. The opening session was on May 10, 1775, in the Pennsylvania State House. This time, the delegates had to face the dangerous question of revolution. John Hancock was chosen as president of the Congress, and George Washington was named commander-in-chief of the new Continental Army.

Like many American families, the Griscoms and the Rosses had split loyalties. Betsy's parents, and those relatives who were still Quakers, refused even to consider rebellion. On the other hand, Betsy's older sister and husband, Sarah and William Donaldson, were Patriots. Although Betsy considered herself a Patriot, she had been a Quaker too long not to sympathize with her Quaker family and neighbors. Feelings in Philadelphia ran so high against Quakers that many were afraid to leave their homes.

Most of John's relatives were Patriots. John had three uncles who were delegates to both the First and Second Continental Congresses: George Ross, George Read, and Edward Biddle. However, the uncle whom John had been named after, John Ross, was a staunch Loyalist.

Everywhere that Betsy went in Philadelphia, she saw signs of war. She noticed all sorts of new flags, the "Don't Tread on Me" Rattlesnake flag, New England's Pine Tree flag, and the white Rhode Island flag with its blue anchor and thirteen stars. Swords, pistols, muskets, and knapsacks filled hardware shop windows. Men lined up to join the militia in front of the city's taverns. Open lots were turned into parade grounds. Even from her shop, Betsy could hear the shrill piping of fifes and the roll of drums that went on from early morning until dusk.

On June 23, 1775, George Washington marched his troops out of Philadelphia. Hundreds of citizens like Betsy and John gathered along Second Street to cheer on the American forces as they headed for Massachusetts. It was a gala occasion, with bands playing and flags waving.

As part of the war effort, John Ross continued his Citizen Guard duty along the waterfront. The sound of water lapping against the pilings and a raw wind sweeping off the Delaware River made for cold and lonely nights. At least when he completed his rounds, he could return to a warm home. And he still had his work. The Philadelphia tax rolls for 1775 listed him as "John Ross Upholder."

Betsy was lonely during those nights when John was gone. She was left to tidy up the shop, bank the fires, and lock the shutters and doors. She missed their evenings together, finishing last minute tasks, reading out loud to one another, or just talking over the day's events. But Betsy had never been a complainer, and she didn't complain now.

CHAPTER 8

One winter night, shortly before dawn, Betsy was startled awake by a knock on the front door. She reached out to feel John's side of the bed. It was empty. John wasn't home yet from patrol duty. Maybe he was locked out.

Betsy pulled on her robe and hurried down the winding, narrow staircase and across the cold shop floor. She unlocked and opened the front door. Because the watchman hadn't yet trimmed the whale oil lamps along Arch Street, she could see that it wasn't John who had knocked. Instead, a knot of men stood clustered together as if for warmth.

The men avoided Betsy's eyes. Then the little group parted. Several men stepped forward carrying a limp figure. It was John! With her heartbeat filling her chest, Betsy held the door open and stepped back.

Carrying the unconscious form of her husband into the house, the men tried to explain. John had been making his rounds on Water Street. . . . There had been an explosion and John had been hurt. . . . They had brought him here. . . . Maybe she should send for a doctor.

Stunned, Betsy led the little procession up the stairs. The lamp flame flickered in her trembling hand. The men carefully laid John on the bed, then backed out of the room.

Betsy forced herself to stay calm. What should she do first? She was known up and down Arch Street for her medical skills. She had treated sick neighbors for all sorts of ailments and fevers. Unlike most of Philadelphia's doctors, she had never put much faith in either calomel as a drug or bleeding the patient. Instead, she crushed herbs that she had dried herself and combined them with powders and compounds from the apothecary shop. Now she would need to draw on all her knowledge.

Over the next few days, John regained consciousness, but he didn't regain his strength or health. Betsy tried to keep the shop going, but her heart wasn't in it.

She spent every free moment by John's side as he slowly grew weaker. Nothing she did seemed to help. Even the doctor she called in could do little.

One day blended into another, and John grew worse. In January, Betsy's birthday came and went without notice. And then it was over. All of Betsy's love, medicines, and prayers were to no avail, and John died.

The church bells tolled as John Ross was buried in the Christ Church Burial Grounds on a blustery January day. Although Betsy was surrounded by relatives, friends, and John's family, she was numb with grief. With no tombstone marking John's grave, the only memorial was a line in the Christ Church Burial Book: "January 21, 1776 John Ross (upholsterer) C. C."

A little more than two years after their marriage, and three weeks after her twenty-fourth birthday, Betsy Griscom Ross found herself a widow.

CHAPTER 9

It was an unhappy winter for Betsy, gray, bleak, and cold. In the daytime, measuring, cutting, hemming, mending, and meeting with customers kept her busy. But the winter afternoons darkened early, making the lonely nights seem endless.

During those long nights, Betsy considered her choices. Her parents wanted her to move back in with them, and she was tempted. To be surrounded by a loving family would feel safe. On the other hand, Betsy knew that her parents would try to talk her into rejoining the Society of Friends. They might even urge her to give up the upholstery business that she and John had struggled so hard to get started.

Another choice was to return to John Webster's Upholstery Shop. Betsy knew that she was good at what she did. Friend Webster would be happy to hire her back, and this time she would demand a salary.

Betsy decided against both choices. Hadn't Great Aunt Sarah always pushed her to be independent? Going home or back to Webster's would be too easy. If Great Aunt Sarah had run a business alone, then so could she. And if John were alive, Betsy was sure that he would want her to carry on with their shop.

During that long, sad winter, the house next door became vacant. Betsy's neighbor had been a shoemaker, and his front room would be perfect for her upholstery shop. The narrow, steep-roofed brick house, with its cream-colored trim, was similar to the one she was in. But a lovely locust tree grew out front, which would provide shade during Philadelphia's hot summers.

Betsy signed the lease, packed up her belongings, and carted them next door to 89 Arch Street. She scrubbed the front room and set up her shop. She would live in the rest of the house. A hallway joined the front room and the back parlor. Two narrow staircases at either end of the hall led to the upstairs bedchambers. The front bedchamber would be hers, while the back bedchamber would serve as her work room. There was a kitchen, pantry, and plenty of storage space in the cellar, with the necessary, or outhouse, in the backyard.

Betsy continued to attend Christ Church, where she had made good friends. Johanna Ross, John's younger sister, was one of them. Johanna and "Sister Betsy" had always gotten along well, and after John's death, they became even closer. John's three uncles, who were delegates to the Second Continental Congress, worshiped at Christ Church, too.

Betsy remembered the three Claypoole sisters, Susannah, Martha, and Clarissa Sidney, from her school days. They were faithful members of Christ Church, and as Betsy came to know them better, their laughter cheered her up. Betsy also knew their brother. John Claypoole had shown an interest in her until she told him that she cared for John Ross. Now John Claypoole was away on militia duty.

January and February of 1776 slowly gave way to March and April. The short dreary days of winter began to lengthen, and Betsy's spirits picked up with the coming warmth. Wide V's of honking geese flew high overhead on their way north. Fresh, moist breezes wafted off the Delaware and Schuylkill Rivers. White snowdrops poked through the melting snow, followed first by crocuses and then by daffodils and tulips. The heavily scented blossoms on the locust tree out front filled Betsy's house with a wonderful fragrance.

With the arrival of spring, the pace of the war quickened. George Washington's troops had successfully kept Boston under siege, and the British abandoned the city in March. The American forces had not fared so well in Canada, where they had been badly beaten. Because the next possible British target was New York City, the Second Continental Congress decided that it was time to meet with the commander-in-chief.

General George Washington arrived in Philadelphia on May 23, 1776. A delegate wrote: "Yesterday, about two o'clock P.M., came into [town] from New York, General Washington, as did his lady, the day before."

Most traffic arriving from the north traveled down Second Street, only a block or so from Betsy's house. If

Betsy didn't see either General or Mrs. Washington come into town, she no doubt heard about their arrival from a neighbor.

General Washington had bad news for Congress. They were in for a long and difficult war, and he desperately needed more troops, arms, and supplies. But without the power to tax the people, Congress had no way to raise money. Serious as the war situation was, Washington had something else on his mind. He was concerned about a national flag.

Even though the country was at war, each colony continued to act in its own interests. Virginians made fun of New Englanders as being peasants and shopkeepers. New Englanders mocked Virginians as being lazy squires. Pennsylvanians called Virginians snobbish and Bostonians mobbish. Washington hoped that a national flag would unite the colonies and become a symbol of their common purpose.

Washington had already tried to adopt a national flag, the Grand Union flag. It had seven red and six white stripes. In the flag's upper left quarter, called the canton, was a small copy of the British national flag. As time went on, the Grand Union flag caused more problems than it solved. The British national flag in the canton sent the message that the colonies were

still loyal to the king. Furthermore, the Grand Union flag, which was also flown by American ships, was almost the same as the hated British East India Company flag.

George Washington, who had plans for a new national flag, decided to work with a small committee of three: two congressmen and himself. Congressman George Ross had become good friends with George Washington during the First Continental Congress. Congressman Robert Morris, who was the wealthy owner of a large fleet of ships, was eager for his vessels to fly an original American flag.

George Ross had an idea. His nephew's widow was the perfect person to make the flag. She was a fine young woman and a skilled seamstress. George Ross told Washington that Betsy Ross was a true Patriot of good character. She could be trusted to sew the flag without a word to anyone. George Washington was interested. They would meet with Mistress Ross as soon as possible.

CHAPTER 10

Betsy started her day much like any other. After she drew water from the neighborhood well, she ate a breakfast of porridge, applesauce, and corncakes. She cleaned up her kitchen, tidied the house, and opened the shutters to let in the smells and sounds of a lovely spring morning. Most of May had been wet and cool. Now warm sunlight flooded her shop. More than five months had passed since John's death. Betsy was feeling more like her old self.

There was always traffic on Arch Street. Betsy pulled her chair over to the window as she worked. Pedestrians hurried by on errands. Street peddlers sang out their wares. Wagons, carts, coaches, and carriages bumped and clattered over the cobblestones.

Betsy looked up and saw three distinguished-looking gentlemen approaching the house.

Betsy recognized all of them. Uncle George Ross, of course, was a familiar figure. And everyone in Philadelphia knew the wealthy businessman Robert Morris by sight. As for their companion, he was taller than the others. Broad-shouldered and handsomely dressed, with freshly powdered hair, the third man was the person all Philadelphia was talking about, General George Washington.

Betsy hurried to the door and opened it. The three men removed their three-cornered hats, greeted her, and entered. Signs of Betsy's trade were everywhere. The upholstered chair was still displayed in the front window. A sofa pillow was half-stuffed with horsehair. Muslin curtains were draped over a chair. Pattern books, ledger books, and sketches were stacked on Betsy's desk. Trying her best not to appear flustered, Betsy invited the men into her back parlor. The shop was too public a place to talk.

Betsy's parlor, with its flowered wallpaper and freshly sanded floor, was simple and neat. It was a pleasant room with a tall chest, a few chairs, a gateleg table, and a looking glass. A corner cupboard was filled with Betsy's prize possessions, books, pewter pieces, and glassware. The fireplace was framed in cheerful blue tiles and covered by a handsome fire-screen that Betsy had embroidered.

The three men didn't waste any time. General Washington pulled a chair up to the table and sat down. Taking out a piece of paper, he unfolded it. Could Mistress Ross copy the flag in the picture?

Betsy studied the rough drawing. Like the Grand Union flag, this flag had red and white stripes. But instead of the British Union Jack in the canton, there were thirteen six-pointed stars. Betsy considered General Washington's request. She had never made a flag before but she saw no reason why she couldn't.

"I'll try," she replied.

Betsy had a good sense of design, and right away she saw how the flag could be improved. She hesitated before giving her opinion to these important gentlemen, but only for a moment. Although she knew that most regimental flags were square, she suggested that this flag be made in the shape of a rectangle. And five-pointed stars would be more practical. To demonstrate, she took a square piece of paper and folded it four different ways. With the scissors from her chatelaine, she made one cut. When she opened the paper, she held up a perfect five-pointed star.

The committee of three agreed with her changes. As General Washington altered his drawing to follow her suggestions, George Ross asked when she could finish the flag. General Washington was leaving Philadelphia soon, and they were in a hurry.

Betsy replied that she would start working immediately and finish as soon as she could. George Ross gave Betsy money for her expenses. Robert Morris told her the name of a ship's merchant who could show her sample flags and outfit her with supplies.

Betsy had a lot to do in very little time. Closing up her shop, she hurried to the shipping merchant's store.

The merchant lent her an old flag. Betsy examined it closely. It was made from wool bunting fabric and had extra rows of stitching with sturdy linen thread. The edges were bound with heavy sailcloth. She could see right away that the flag had been made strong enough to withstand severe winds and weather.

Betsy took great care in measuring and cutting the stripes. But when she began to handstitch them together, she discovered that she needed a different set of needles for the heavy wool bunting and tough sailcloth. Sewing a flag certainly wasn't anything like turning up a lady's silk hem or tacking ruffles on a shirt.

As soon as Betsy was finished, she got in touch with George Ross, who came by to pick up the flag. When he returned the next day, he reported that General Washington had been pleased with her work and had given his approval. George Ross paid Betsy and told her to make as many flags as she could and as quickly as possible. Money would be advanced to her from time to time.

The flag had seven red stripes and six white ones. The canton had thirteen white five-pointed stars arranged in a circle on a blue background, or field. Forever after, the new American flag would be known as the Betsy Ross flag.

CHAPTER 11

Betsy was flattered by her meeting with General Washington and his committee. And she was delighted at the prospect of making flags. She could use all the work she could get.

As for General Washington, by the time he left Philadelphia on June 5, 1776, flags were no longer on his mind. He was making plans to defend New York and Long Island against a British attack.

The Second Continental Congress had its own concerns. For weeks the delegates had been arguing over whether "these United Colonies are, and of right ought to be, free and independent States." Even while the debate continued, Thomas Jefferson, John Adams, Benjamin Franklin, Roger Sherman, and Robert Livingston were writing a document that set forth the reasons for declaring independence from Great Britain. Betsy was as curious as everyone else about what was going on at the State House.

On July 1, the committee of five presented to Congress the document that had been written mainly by Thomas Jefferson. After three more days of making changes, the Second Continental Congress adopted the Declaration of Independence. The United Colonies became the United States. Just as Betsy had been born on the first day of the first year of a new era, July 4, 1776, marked the first day of the first year of a new nation.

On July 8, a public reading of the declaration was held. The bronze bell hanging in the State House tower, which Samuel Griscom had helped to build twenty-three years before, summoned Philadelphia's citizens. The words on the bell, which would one day be known as the Liberty Bell, read: "Proclaim Liberty throughout all the Land unto all the Inhabitants Thereof."

It was a warm and sunny morning as shopkeepers like Betsy Ross, clerks, merchants, housewives, and children hurried to the State House Yard for the noontime reading. Colonel John Nixon read the Declaration of Independence in a booming voice. When he had finished, the people raised a cheer.

"Huzza! Huzza! Huzza!"

Militiamen tore down the king's coat of arms from the State House wall and burned it. Battalions paraded in the Yard. Guns saluted. All that day and well into the night, Philadelphia's bells pealed as the city celebrated. One Philadelphian noted, "Fine starlight, pleasant evening. There were bonfires, ringing bells, with other great demonstrations of joy upon the unanimity and agreement of the declaration."

Unfortunately, the war news coming into Philadelphia was bad. Both Long Island and New York City had fallen to the British. By November 1776, General Washington's Continental troops were fleeing across New Jersey with the British in hot pursuit. Washington and his men didn't reach safety in Pennsylvania until December.

There were rumors that the British were about to invade Philadelphia. Panicked, Congress fled to Baltimore. All businesses and shops like Betsy's were ordered closed. Drums beat. On December 8, 1776, Philadelphia's watchmen announced that martial law was declared. Every man between sixteen and sixty was ordered to take up arms against the British.

Only a few weeks later, Betsy heard about a remarkable American victory. On Christmas night, Washington and his men had rowed across the Delaware from Pennsylvania to New Jersey in a terrible sleet and snowstorm. After landing at 4 A.M. on December 26, they had marched to Trenton, where they had attacked and defeated the Hessian forces. The Hessians were soldiers from Germany who had been hired by the British to fight in America. General Nathanael Greene described how they waged war: "Men slaughtered, Women ravisht, and Houses plundered . . . brutal conduct."

To raise the spirits of Philadelphians, Washington had more than nine hundred Hessian prisoners marched through the city's streets. Philadelphians' spirits were raised a little too high. They almost rioted in their zeal to get at the hated Hessians.

Four days later, Washington and his men again crossed the Delaware River and defeated the British at Princeton, New Jersey. The two American victories had warded off a possible British invasion of Philadelphia. Betsy, along with everyone else, was immensely relieved. Now she could get back to business as usual. If the British had captured the city, who would have ordered upholstery or furnishings? Even worse, if the British had found out about her flag making, she might have been arrested.

Although Betsy kept her shop open, the war made supplies almost impossible to come by. Because firewood was both expensive and scarce, Betsy spent most of her working hours bundled up trying to stay warm as she mended, patched, and repaired what work came in.

With the cold continuing, Betsy carried her foot warmer with her as she attended church and visited her friends, Johanna Ross and the Claypoole sisters. The Claypooles were worried about their brother John in the militia, although he hadn't seen action. Knowing that John had once cared for Betsy, his sisters talked of him often. Betsy had been a widow for a year now and might again consider marriage.

The Claypoole women were in for a disappointment. Betsy did meet another man, but it wasn't John Claypoole.

CHAPTER 12

Like John Claypoole, Joseph Ashburn had been interested in Betsy before her marriage to John Ross. Betsy, Joseph, and John Claypoole had all known each other from their days at Friends Public School. Now Betsy's brother-in-law, William Donaldson, brought the young widow and Joseph Ashburn together again. In the past, William and Joseph had served on the same ship.

As a boy, Joseph had been drawn to the water and boats, and he still was. In 1772, his aunt had given him command of her merchant ship, the *Swallow*. At first, he had sailed the *Swallow* from Philadelphia to the Caribbean Sea in the West Indian trade, bringing back sugar, rum, molasses, spices, and tobacco. Then, when trouble began between the colonies and Great Britain, he became a legal privateersman. The Pennsylvania government granted him the right to seize British ships and their cargoes.

Privateering was risky. British patrol vessels, foreign privateers, and pirates were all on the lookout for merchant ships like the *Swallow*. Although the *Swallow* was fast, she was too small to carry heavy arms.

By early 1777, British vessels guarding Delaware Bay made sailing in and out of Philadelphia difficult and dangerous. Eager as Joseph was to be at sea, he welcomed the chance to spend time in Philadelphia. He was drawn to Betsy and enjoyed calling on her. Betsy was drawn to Joseph, too.

Joseph Ashburn was stocky and muscular and not very tall. As a sailor, it helped to be of average height and size. Below-deck space was cramped and the hatchways were narrow and low.

With Joseph in the city most of the winter, Betsy saw him almost every day. By the time the snow and ice were gone and the spring shad had begun their run up the Delaware and Schuylkill Rivers, Betsy and Joseph had fallen in love.

They decided that June would be a perfect time to be married, and they made plans. Just before their wedding, Betsy received a welcome present, a payment for making naval flags. "An order on William Webb to Elizabeth Ross, for fourteen pounds, twelve shillings, two pence for making ships colors and put into William Richards' stores," read the May 29, 1777, Pennsylvania State Navy Board minutes.

On June 15, Betsy and Joseph traveled a mile south of the city to Wicaco, an Indian name meaning "peaceful place." There they were married in the Gloria Dei Lutheran Church. The church's Book of Marriage recorded the happy event. "Joseph Ashburn and Elizabeth Ross, June the 15th, by Licence."

A "peaceful place" was an appropriate setting for Betsy and Joseph's wedding. This time Betsy didn't have to sneak away at night to keep her marriage a secret from her parents. She didn't need to find a backer to post money for a marriage bond, or ask an old friend to arrange for a justice of the peace. Instead, the ceremony was witnessed by family and friends, with Sarah and William Donaldson once again Betsy's main supporters.

By coincidence, the day before Betsy and Joseph's wedding, the Second Continental Congress passed a flag resolution. The flag that Betsy had made for George Washington the year before became the official flag of the United States. The congressional secretary had

hastily written the June fourteenth resolution in the official minutes with cross-outs and corrections.

"Resolved That the Flag of the united states be 13 stripes alternate red and white, that the Union be 13 stars white in a blue field representing a new constellation."

Each state was to supply flags for its own military units. At first, Washington was more concerned with using the flag to identify ships at sea than he was in using it for the army. As a result, the army flew hundreds of different national, regimental, battalion, company, and troop flags.

All of Betsy's flags had the traditional arrangement of stars and stripes. Because the flag resolution hadn't described the design of the flag, other flag makers turned out flags pretty much as they pleased. They placed the thirteen stars in circles, squares, or rows, with the stars having anywhere from five to eight points. Although some flags had seven red and six white stripes,

others had seven white stripes and six red. Still others had extra stripes or even blue stripes. Many flag makers added eagles, scrolls, the number "76," or other symbols of the new nation.

Only a few weeks after Betsy and Joseph were married, a Philadelphia newspaper reported a special event. "Last Friday the 4th of July, being the Anniversary of the Independence of the United States of America, was celebrated in this city with demonstrations of joy and festivity. About noon all the armed ships and gallies on the river were drawn up before the city, dressed in the gayest manner, with colours of the United States and streamers displayed."

Now that Betsy was turning out mostly naval flags, the ships' "colours" no doubt came from her shop. Betsy didn't care whether she made navy flags or army flags. They all helped the war effort. And they were all good for business.

She and Joseph had decided early on that she would continue working. She wouldn't ask Joseph to give up the sea, and he wouldn't ask her to give up her shop. Besides, Joseph would be gone for long periods of time. She had too much ambition and energy to sit home quietly while he was away. As long as customers knocked on her door, she would keep her shop open.

CHAPTER 13

Not long after Betsy and Joseph's marriage in June 1777, Joseph slipped past the British blockade in the *Swallow* and headed for the West Indies. Although Betsy had known that he would leave sooner or later, it was hard not to worry. There were also rumors that the British army's next target was Philadelphia. The capital was an important seaport and would be a prize for the British.

The rumors were true. Some seventeen thousand British and Hessian soldiers landed in Maryland only sixty miles south of Philadelphia and started north. Once again, the city was in a turmoil. The Second Continental Congress talked of leaving the city. Patriots buried their silver and valuables and packed up in case they had to flee.

Washington was camped with his troops six miles northwest of Philadelphia in Germantown. Now he made immediate plans to march south to stop the enemy. But to ease the fears of Philadelphians, he would parade his men through the city in a show of strength and spirit.

On August 24, 1777, eleven thousand militiamen and Continental soldiers marched through Philadelphia playing "Yankee Doodle Dandy" on their fifes and drums. Because there was still no money for uniforms, the men were dressed in a mixture of rough brown, blue, and buff homespun. Some wore white rifle shirts and leggings. To give them a unified look, Washington ordered his troops to tuck a sprig of greenery into their cocked hats.

During that same month of August, Joseph came home. Betsy was overjoyed to see him. But all too soon he was off again in the *Swallow*. Joseph had been assigned to deliver supplies to the two American forts that guarded the Port of Philadelphia. Fort Mifflin was nine miles south of the city on Mud Island. Fort Mercer was directly across the Delaware River at Red Bank, New Jersey. Merchant ships, like the *Swallow*, and the Pennsylvania State Navy's row galleys kept the two forts supplied.

Joseph was gone a good deal of the time, and when he was in port, he was usually working on the *Swallow*. He repaired the sails and rigging, spliced lines, dug seaworms out of the hull, checked the caulking, and arranged for food, water, rum, supplies, and ammunition to be loaded for his next run.

Betsy sometimes packed up a picnic and carried it

down to the waterfront to share with Joseph. Even with all the ships coming and going, she noticed that the Pennsylvania State Navy flags were gradually being replaced by the Stars and Stripes. She felt a sense of pride that most of those Stars and Stripes had been made right in her shop.

CHAPTER 14

In the fall of 1777, the war came ever closer to Philadelphia. On September 11, the Americans under George Washington and the British under Commander-in-Chief General William Howe fought at Brandywine Creek just twenty-five miles southwest of the city.

Philadelphia was complete bedlam. Smug Loyalists began to return. Patriots took flight in wagons piled high with their belongings. Congressmen fled seventy miles west to Lancaster, Pennsylvania, and from Lancaster to York. A young woman told of "wagons rattling, horses galloping, women running, children crying, delegates flying, and altogether the greatest consternation, fright and terror that can be imagined."

The Delaware River was crowded with Patriots in rowboats or any craft they could find that would get them to New Jersey. Joseph had to leave, too. He not only had to save the *Swallow,* but he was also a privateersman and his life was at risk. If the British seized Philadelphia and he was captured, he would be sent to prison . . . or worse.

Betsy had no idea when she would see her husband again. But she had been alone before and had managed, and she would manage this time, too.

By the end of the day, the Americans had lost the

Battle of the Brandywine and were in full retreat after suffering hundreds of casualties. Betsy heard from the Claypoole sisters that their brother John had fought in the battle. He must have done well. He had been commissioned a second lieutenant.

For the next ten days, the British army kept the pressure on the American troops. At 1 A.M. on September 21, 1777, they charged an American force at Paoli, Pennsylvania, with bayonets. The attack was so vicious that it became known as the Paoli Massacre.

All along their route, the British and Hessian soldiers stole pigs and poultry, slaughtered cattle, and robbed apple orchards. British General Howe, who camped in Germantown with his main forces, sent General Lord Charles Cornwallis and four battalions down Germantown Road to occupy Philadelphia.

The British and Hessian soldiers under Cornwallis followed the same route that Washington's men had taken the month before. This time Betsy didn't greet the incoming army with waves and cheers. Like everyone else, she locked herself in her house. Even behind closed doors, she could hear the strains of "God Save the King," the rumble of artillery trains, and the clatter of mounted dragoons on the cobblestones. She could follow the soldiers' route by the sound of their marching boots as they swung onto Second Street and crossed Arch Street close to her house.

A Philadelphian woman wrote: "They looked well, clean and well clad, and the contrast between them and our own poor bare-footed, ragged troops was very great and caused a feeling of despair."

It was true. Unlike the Americans, with their brave little sprigs of green, the enemy troops appeared well-fed and well-clothed. The British wore scarlet uniforms and cone-shaped hats. The Hessians, in their blue uniforms with black trim, carried handsome black silk flags with gold lettering.

Philadelphia was closed down. Houses and shops were shuttered and locked. Bells from the State House,

Christ Church, and St. Peter's Church had been smuggled out of the city so that the enemy couldn't melt them down to make cannons. Though many of the Patriots had left, most of the Quakers stayed. Betsy stayed, too. She couldn't ensure Joseph's safety or her own, but she was determined to stand guard over their home in the face of the enemy.

CHAPTER 15

With fabrics of any kind in short supply, Betsy kept her shop going the best she could. Fortunately, even the wealthy Loyalist ladies had to make do with the clothes they already owned. Betsy mended and patched their elegant gowns, sewing on what ribbons, bows, and laces she had on hand.

Betsy found it hard to keep her mind on business. So far, she hadn't heard from Joseph. She didn't know his whereabouts or even if he was safe. She could only pray that no news was good news.

There was very little good news to go around. Although the Loyalists invited British officers to stay in their homes, the British army was short of beds. Furthermore, General Howe was preparing to move his main army to Philadelphia from Germantown. To find quarters for his men, Howe ordered Cornwallis to take a census of every house in the city.

Two redcoated soldiers came to Betsy's house and knocked. Betsy did her best to appear calm and courteous. The soldiers were equally courteous. How many rooms in her house? How many people in the household? Their ages and nationalities? Her occupation?

Even to a soldier's untrained eye, Betsy's trade was obvious. Betsy wore her scissors and needle cushion on her chatelaine. A threadbare bedhanging lay over a workbench with her sewing basket beside it. Gowns, waistcoats, and ruffled shirts ready to be mended or altered were neatly hung up. And the redcoats could see that the house was too small to be useful. It was hard for Betsy not to let out a sigh of relief as they left.

Cornwallis reported to Howe that there were six thousand houses in Philadelphia occupied by nearly twenty-four thousand people. Five hundred and forty houses were empty. When Howe's troops arrived, Philadelphia was going to be a very crowded city.

General Washington, however, had no intention of letting Howe move his main forces into the city. He would attack and defeat the British at Germantown, march down Germantown Road and free Philadelphia.

At dawn on October 4, 1777, Betsy was awakened by booming gunfire. The battle of Germantown had begun. Neighbors in all stages of dress and undress rushed from their houses. Although the street lights were still lit, there was such a thick fog that it was impossible to see more than ten feet away.

News of the battle soon reached Philadelphia. Despite the heavy fog, the fighting had gone well at first, with several British troops in full retreat. Then redcoats had taken over Chief Justice Benjamin Chew's mansion and held their position against American attack. But the fog and haze of gunsmoke had caused confusion. Two American divisions each thought the other was the enemy, and they both retreated. When they realized their mistake, they tried to regroup. It was too late and they were forced to withdraw. The British were victorious.

Casualties were high on both sides. Nearly seven hundred Americans and more than five hundred British were killed or wounded. Four hundred Americans were taken prisoner. Before long, farm wagons filled with the dead and dying came bumping down Germantown Road into a horrified city.

Because Pennsylvania Hospital couldn't begin to

handle all the wounded, the State House, churches, public buildings, and private homes opened their doors. Betsy, with her gift of healing, hurried to help, along with hundreds of other women. They nursed both American and British wounded, assisted in surgery, and made bandages. They cooked soups and stews and brought in blankets and clothing from their own homes. The Quakers, especially, outdid themselves in caring for the wounded.

Meanwhile, families gathered at the State House, desperate for word of their loved ones. The Claypooles were heartsick to learn that John had been seriously wounded. An iron gun carriage had exploded and a flying fragment had pierced his side. Bleeding badly, he had been carried back to camp by his comrades.

Betsy and the other women may have wanted to help the Americans in the Walnut Street Prison, but there was nothing they could do. The prisoners were allowed no visitors, medical care, or food from the outside. For five days the men were without rations, blankets, or fuel. All too often Betsy saw the redcoated prison guards bury the American dead in a common trench.

Betsy was physically and emotionally exhausted.

Nursing the wounded and dying men, and watching the parade of hasty burials was almost more than she could bear. Joseph was constantly in her thoughts and prayers. If only she could know that he was safe.

CHAPTER 16

Life in Philadelphia seemed to go from bad to worse. The enemy troops looted jewelry, watches, paintings, silverware, and household goods. A Philadelphia Quaker, Elizabeth Drinker, wrote in her journal: "These are sad times for Thieving and plundering, tis hardly safe to leave the door open a minute."

Food supplies dwindled. Betsy spent hours just trying to find something to buy that she could afford. Any beef in the market was $1 a pound and usually rotten. A pound of butter that had cost 13 cents two years before now cost $1.

The situation was just as serious for the British. Washington still guarded the roads to the north. The only way the British could get food and supplies into Philadelphia was to open the Delaware River for shipping. That meant destroying the two American forts that guarded the city, Fort Mifflin and Fort Mercer. They would also have to remove two rows of iron spikes that the Americans had planted in the river. The spikes were designed to rip open the bottom of any ship that sailed over them. Furthermore, the British had to act quickly, before the river froze for the winter.

On October 12, 1777, a British vessel removed a section of iron spikes, opening a ninety-foot-wide gap in the channel. It was just wide enough for a ship to sail through.

Finally, after five days of brutal shelling by the British, Fort Mifflin fell. Once the Americans at Fort Mifflin surrendered, there was no saving Fort Mercer across the river. It, too, was abandoned. At last the British controlled the Delaware River all the way to Philadelphia.

As armed British warships began to patrol up and down the river, Betsy was frantic for word of Joseph. At last she heard that both he and the *Swallow* were safe. Along with all other American ships, Joseph had been ordered to hide the *Swallow* in New Jersey's little coves and inlets.

Joseph might as well have been on the moon. Betsy couldn't get word to him and he couldn't get word to her. She just had to be satisfied that he was out of danger, and she hoped that he knew she was safe, too.

During that winter of 1777–78, Betsy had no way to keep her house warm. With firewood impossible to find, the water in her bedside basin froze every night. Her hands were so cold that she could hardly thread a needle. Philadelphia's poor were even worse off. The British army, which was using the Alms House as a barracks, had thrown the homeless into the streets.

Although British and Hessian soldiers broke up furniture, doors, gates, and church pews for firewood, their commander-in-chief wasn't suffering in the least. General Howe, who rode around town in a handsome coach, was wined and dined at Loyalist dinners, balls, receptions, concerts, and the theater.

As a result, Betsy had more work than she'd had in some time. Now that the Delaware River was open to British ships, fabrics began to arrive from England. Because Loyalist women were the only ones who could afford new gowns, Betsy put her talents to dressmaking. Much to her distaste, she also tailored and mended British officers' uniforms. It was said that some of the soldiers called her "Little Rebel."

Although Philadelphia's Patriots suffered shortages, they were better off than the ragged American troops camped for the winter at Valley Forge. One soldier summed up the wretched conditions: "Here all is confusion—smoke and cold—hunger and filthyness—a pox on my bad luck."

Betsy and other Philadelphians did their best to help the American soldiers only twenty miles away. The Claypooles were especially concerned when they heard that John was at Valley Forge. As Betsy packed up boots, shoes, stockings, medicines, food, and clothing, she hoped that some of them would find their way to her old friend from school days.

CHAPTER 17

The opening months of 1778 weren't any better than the closing months of 1777. Betsy was still without word from Joseph. And like everyone else, she still struggled to find food, firewood, and a way to make ends meet. General Howe, his officers, and their Loyalist friends carried on as usual, too, with parties, balls, and theater-going.

As winter finally ended and spring arrived, Betsy heard that British ships were searching New Jersey coves and inlets for American vessels. Betsy did her best to find out what was happening. She didn't care whether it was gossip, rumors, or idle talk, as long as there was news one way or the other. Fortunately, the news was good. All merchant ships, including the

Swallow, had escaped across the Delaware River and were safely anchored in Pennsylvania. With the British still in Philadelphia, Joseph couldn't come home. But at least he was safe. For the time being, that was enough.

The British search for American vessels in New Jersey turned up only a few small craft. Merchant ships, like the *Swallow,* had slipped away. The navy had stripped its ships of sails, rigging, guns, and stores. The ships had then been sunk in creeks to be raised when the danger was past.

In May, the party-loving Howe was replaced as commander-in-chief of the British army by Sir Henry Clinton. Just before Howe left for London, his staff put on a farewell gala in his honor that was called a *meschianza,* an Italian word meaning "mixture or medley."

On the afternoon of May 18, 1778, British and Hessian officers and four hundred Loyalist guests boarded thirty barges at the Philadelphia docks. Cannons saluted and military bands played "God Save the King" as the little fleet sailed a mile down the Delaware River.

Two huge tents had been set up on the lawns of a large estate. Ladies in beautiful costumes clapped as their special "knights" jousted in mock tournaments. Afterward, a banquet of some twelve hundred dishes was served in a brilliant hall of mirrors. Feasting, drinking, dancing, and gambling continued until dawn.

Just a month later, Betsy awoke on a hot and rainy June 18 to find that the British army was gone. All the British ships had left, too, taking three thousand Loyalists with them. London had ordered a complete withdrawal from Philadelphia.

Being free of the British was like a second Declaration of Independence. Men crowded the taverns to celebrate. Neighbors no longer had to whisper for fear of being overheard. Gaunt figures emerged from the Walnut Street Prison, blinking in the bright June sunlight. Flags reappeared. Betsy could go back to making flags. Best of all, Joseph would be coming home.

CHAPTER 18

Early in the summer of 1778, Joseph came running up Arch Street from the waterfront. He was home at last. Even the *Swallow* was safe and tied up at her usual mooring at the foot of Race Street. During the year that Betsy and Joseph had been married, they had been apart for nine months. Now they could finally spend some time together.

If life for the Ashburns was returning to normal, life in Philadelphia was not. The British navy was blockading the entrance to the Delaware River. Supplies and provisions were still scarce and terribly expensive.

Even worse, the British had left behind mountains of rubbish. Betsy could hardly pick her way through

the reeking filth as she made her market rounds. She had been lucky that her house had been too small to house British soldiers. Some of the British had simply thrown their garbage into the cellars. When they could no longer stand the smell, they had tossed it in the streets. Flies swarmed everywhere. Windows were shattered or boarded up. The State House and the churches were unusable.

When Patriots who had fled the city began to return, conditions gradually improved. Betsy was pleased to see wagonful after wagonful of garbage carted off the streets. She could hear the racket of rebuilding all over town. The State House and church bells were brought back from hiding. Their familiar pealing reminded everyone that the hated British were gone.

But Betsy wasn't happy when Joseph again set sail for the West Indies as a privateersman. British vessels had stepped up their patrols. Gales and storms on the West Indian voyages could be fierce, and the *Swallow* was getting old.

For the next year, Joseph sailed the *Swallow* between Philadelphia and the West Indies. Betsy's heart was in her throat every time he left, and was filled with joy and thanksgiving when he docked. She was pregnant now with their first child, and that added to her concern. Still, prices of everything had soared, and they could certainly use the money he earned. Beef was up to $5 a pound and firewood cost $150 a cord.

Besides running the shop, Betsy worked for the army loading cartridges with powder and musket balls. She was not only paid, but she also had the satisfaction of knowing that she was saving the soldiers precious time on the battlefield.

On September 15, 1779, Betsy gave birth to a daughter. Betsy and Joseph named the baby Lucilla, but they called her Zilla. Happily, Betsy's business had grown so much that from time to time she hired seamstresses to help. Now, the extra hands in the shop gave Betsy time to spend with her baby.

Another year went by, and Joseph finally had to

admit that the *Swallow* was no longer seaworthy. When a Philadelphia shipping firm offered him the command of a new and larger ship, he eagerly accepted. But the ship wasn't finished, and Joseph agreed to sail to the West Indies under Captain Francis Knox on a fine new brigantine, the *Patty*. Captain Knox was an old friend, and the two men had sailed together before.

The *Patty* was due to leave in October 1780. A voyage to the West Indies usually took about six weeks. Although Betsy was pregnant again, the new baby wasn't due until February. Joseph was sure to be back before then. Still, as Betsy watched Joseph pack, she was uneasy. Privateering was a dangerous game.

O ctober and November were always Betsy's busiest months. Fall was soap- and candle-making season. It was also the season for drying apples and baking apple tarts and pies. Besides her kitchen work, Betsy had the usual shop orders to fill and cartridges to load for the army.

Staying busy was fine with Betsy. It made the time pass quickly. She was so tired at night that she fell right to sleep before troubled thoughts of Joseph filled her head.

But November came and went and there was no sign of Joseph. Betsy tried to reassure herself. Sometimes a run to the West Indies took seven weeks or more. Joseph and Captain Knox were both skilled seamen. The *Patty* was a new, well-built brigantine and far more seaworthy than the old *Swallow*. Nevertheless, it was hard not to worry.

Betsy knew that other seamen were in touch with shipping news. She would ask the sea captains and merchant shippers who hung out at the Coffee House and the Crooked Billet, if they knew anything about the *Patty*.

The men told Betsy more than she might have wanted to hear. Although they didn't know anything about the *Patty*, they reported that the British had tightened their blockade and picked up a lot of American ships. Unusually bad storms had been battering the coast, too.

The Claypooles were also concerned. Their brother John had resigned from the army and shipped out as a privateersman just a short time after Joseph had left. There had been no word of him since.

Betsy was not only pregnant, but she was also coping with almost impossible living conditions. The army's demands for food, firewood, and supplies had brought about terrible shortages and sky-high prices. It didn't help that the Second Continental Congress was issuing almost worthless paper money. A pound of butter, which had cost $1 in 1777, now cost $15, while a loaf of bread was $4. Many Philadelphians were close to starving.

During the harsh winter months, Betsy struggled to keep her house warm and have food enough for Zilla and herself. And then, on a bitterly cold February day, Betsy went into labor. Her time had come. She delivered her second child, a healthy baby girl whom she named Eliza on February 25, 1781. If only Joseph could have been home with his family.

CHAPTER 20

Betsy spent her days caring for her daughters and doing what she could to keep the shop open. Finding food and firewood continued to be a struggle. But finally, there was good news. The British under General Cornwallis surrendered at Yorktown in October 1781. The war was over.

As the months went by, there was still no word from Joseph. Betsy tried to stay cheerful for her two girls. On July 4, 1782, she closed her shop. She dressed Zilla and Eliza in their best and celebrated Independence Day with the rest of Philadelphia. All the city bells rang. Flags flew, drums and fifes played, rockets and fireworks filled the night sky, and a grand reception was held in the State House.

Only five weeks later, Betsy heard that John Claypoole was back in the United States. His ship had been captured by a British vessel and he had been jailed in an English prison. Joseph and John Claypoole had shipped out the same month. Maybe Joseph had been a prisoner and was on his way home, too. Overjoyed at the possibility, Betsy swept up Zilla and Eliza in her arms, hugging and kissing them.

On a hot August fifteenth, Betsy answered a knock on her door. John Claypoole had come to call. Betsy had no way of knowing, but it was John's thirtieth birthday. She greeted him enthusiastically, congratulated him on his safe return, and invited him in. As soon as they were seated in her back parlor she noticed his somber expression. He was pale and thin, but it was more than that.

John plunged right in. Joseph's ship, the *Patty*, had been captured by the British, he told her. Joseph, like John, had been sent to Old Mill Prison in Plymouth, England, where they had found each other. This past February Joseph had fallen ill, and he passed away in March. Conscious and clear-minded to the end, he had died with courage and dignity.

John didn't stay long, just long enough to make sure that Betsy would be all right.

But Betsy wasn't all right. She was shattered. She hadn't even had the comfort of being with her husband when he died.

As the days went by, Betsy managed to smile and appear cheerful with customers, but she shed many private tears. Tired as she was, she found it hard to sleep. In the end, Betsy's work sustained her, as it always had. And she knew how much Zilla and Eliza needed her.

John called on Betsy from time to time, and Betsy found it comforting to talk about Joseph. Together they laughed about Joseph's daredevil antics in school, his love of the water, and the way he had enjoyed racing his catboat. But the talk wasn't always about Joseph. Betsy was interested in hearing about John, too.

John told her how he had crossed the Atlantic on

the privateer *Luzerne*. After reaching France eight weeks later, he had fallen desperately ill. A French family had taken him in and nursed him back to health. In April 1781, the *Luzerne* had been captured by a British ship on her return voyage to Philadelphia.

Landing in Ireland, John and his fellow crew members had been placed in irons and marched seventy miles overland. Thrown into the hold of a prison ship, they had sailed from Ireland to Plymouth, England. Charged with high treason, they had been jailed in Old Mill Prison.

John didn't mention the overcrowded conditions, the cold, the lack of food, the illnesses. Instead, he told Betsy how Joseph and he had supported each other. He described how he had hidden his notebook and kept a secret diary. In the end, John had been one of the lucky ones. He and more than two hundred other prisoners had been sent back to the United States on a prisoner exchange ship.

Betsy enjoyed getting to know John, not as the boy she remembered, but as the adult he had become. His experiences had matured him in the same way that her experiences had matured her. John was tall and handsome, with a strong sense of compassion and caring for those less fortunate. Coming from an educated and successful family, he was well-read, intelligent, and curious about the world around him.

John had been gone for almost two years. He had no job and didn't know what he would do. His family tannery business had failed. And he didn't want to go back to his cousin's print shop, where he had worked after the army. He needed time and room to sort out his future. Only the sea could give him that.

Two months after arriving home, John left for the West Indies on the *Hyder Alley*. He told Betsy that he would probably continue to ship out. Privateering was risky, but the money was good. He might very well make the sea his life's work.

With two daughters to think of, Betsy decided that she would be foolish to become involved with another seafaring man. She couldn't bear the long separations or the worry when a ship was overdue. If John made a career of the sea, they could certainly be friends. But she would never allow their friendship to become anything more.

CHAPTER 21

Betsy had been a Quaker too long not to be plainspoken. She never used fancy words to cover up what was in her heart. She told John Claypoole just how she felt.

John had a decision to make. He was thirty and it was time that he settled down. He admired Betsy's spirit and courage and had come to love her. And he was fond of Zilla and Eliza. Life as a sailor appealed to him, but if he followed the sea, he would lose Betsy.

As John thought about his future, he continued to ship out. Between his runs to the West Indies, he called on Betsy. Although she was always delighted to see him, she kept him at a friendly distance.

It wasn't until summer had passed into fall, fall into

winter, and winter into spring that John finally came to a decision. He would give up the sea and find a job in Philadelphia.

On May 8, 1783, Elizabeth Griscom Ross Ashburn and John Claypoole were married at Christ Church in the company of Zilla, Eliza, close friends, and family. Because they were married on a Thursday, the bride and groom both had to work the next day. John had promised to find a job in Philadelphia, and he had. His new job was right on Arch Street, in Betsy's shop.

Betsy was delighted to teach John the ins and outs of upholstering and flag making. To her surprise, John was just as helpful to her. He brought both his soldiering and seagoing background to the business. The shop began to produce and repair tents, camp beds, camp chairs, cots, and knapsacks for the army. It also made and repaired ships' mattresses, sea beds, tables, and stools. From having worked in his family's tannery business, John was an expert in upholstering with leather.

Soon after Betsy and John were married, they left Christ Church and attended Meetings of the Society of Free Quakers. In 1782, Samuel Wetherill had formed the Society for those Quakers who had been disowned during the Revolution. No member of the Free Quakers could be disowned for any reason.

Betsy, and other disowned Quakers, had scattered to different churches. But they missed their Meeting and the quiet simplicity of their faith. Betsy also liked the fact that Quaker women were equal partners in the home, schoolroom, and meeting house.

The Society of Free Quakers appealed to John, too. Like the Quakers, he had always had a calling to help people in need. Besides, he had a Quaker family history. Although his mother and sisters attended Christ Church, earlier Claypooles had been Quakers for generations. In 1784, Betsy and John joined the Society of Free Quakers with Zilla and Eliza.

CHAPTER 22

After the peace treaty with Great Britain was finally signed in 1783, all sorts of fabrics started coming into Philadelphia. The shop was doing well and Betsy and John were doing well, too. On April 3, 1785, Betsy gave birth to her third girl. They named her Clarissa Sidney after John's sister, Betsy's faithful friend. Only a year and a half later, on November 15, 1786, Betsy and John had another girl, Susan.

With a thriving business and four little girls, Zilla and Eliza Ashburn and Clarissa and Susan Claypoole, 89 Arch Street had become much too small. Betsy and John decided to move to a larger house.

John advertised their new address: "Claypoole, John, Upholsterer, Respectfully informs the Public in general, and his Friends and Customers in particular, that he had removed from Arch Street to the Southwest corner of Race and Second Streets, where he continues to carry on the business of Upholsterer In all its various branches, and on as reasonable terms as are possible to live by."

Betsy's great-grandfather, Andrew Griscom, had built the house in 1683. Known as Griscom's "antiquated" construction, it was one of Philadelphia's earliest brick houses. Although the first colonists had lived in crude log huts and caves, a layer of clay was discovered under the surface of the new settlement that was perfect for making bricks. Some three hundred brick houses had quickly gone up, many of them built by Andrew Griscom.

Betsy and John's move to Second Street came at a time of great sorrow. Betsy and Joseph Ashburn's oldest daughter, Zilla, died. Zilla had been Betsy's first born, the child whose laughter had lifted her spirits when Joseph was missing at sea. Zilla had been her link with Joseph and now Zilla was gone. Betsy remembered her parents' grief when their young children had died. Now she felt the same terrible heartache that only the death of a child can bring.

Soon afterward, Betsy's sister, Sarah Donaldson,

died. For years the two of them had walked to and from school together. From the time they were little, they had exchanged their deepest secrets. Betsy and Sarah had been the closest of sisters.

Despite her pain, Betsy had to work longer and longer hours as shop business continued to grow. John had just landed an important customer, the state government at the Pennsylvania State House. John made furniture for the Council Chamber, upholstered Council Chamber chairs, repaired their venetian blinds, and covered desks.

The shop had earned a fine reputation and had never done better. Except for the heartbreaking loss of Zilla and Sarah Donaldson, the years that Betsy, John, and their girls lived on Second Street were happy.

CHAPTER 23

Betsy had her hands full in the summer of 1787. Eliza was a run-around six-year-old, Clarissa was still a toddler, and baby Susan was just beginning to walk. When Betsy wasn't caring for the children, she was working in the shop.

Philadelphia was a busy place, too. During that hot and humid summer, delegates from all the states, except Rhode Island, met in the State House to discuss the sad condition of the national government. The thirteen states quarreled with each other about boundary lines, tariffs, money, and just about everything else.

The delegates discussed, argued, and disagreed on how the country should be governed. When Betsy did her errands, she saw the delegates clustered in groups.

They stood around after church services and gathered in taverns and coffee houses. Finally, on September 17, 1787, the delegates voted to adopt the Constitution of the United States as the supreme law of the land.

In celebration of both the Constitution and the Fourth of July, on July 4, 1788, Philadelphia put on a gala parade. Marshals led off government officials, uniformed troops, floats, workers carrying the tools of their trade, university students, clergymen, and hundreds more. Betsy and John lined up to watch with other "leftovers" who weren't marching. The following year, the city again celebrated when General Washington was elected the first president of the United States.

In November 1790, Philadelphia became the nation's capital, and the pace of the city picked up. President and Mrs. Washington were seen escorting important visitors around Philadelphia in their handsome carriage. Congress held noisy sessions in the State House. The city taverns and inns were always filled.

Only three years later, Philadelphia was completely shut down when a yellow fever epidemic struck. In the summer of 1793, twenty thousand terror-stricken citizens fled the city. President Washington moved with his household to Germantown. Of those who stayed, nearly one out of five died. Elizabeth Drinker described the horror: "Coffins were kept ready made in piles, near the State House for poor people . . . they dig trenches in the poters-field to bury the dead . . . it is said that many are bury'd after night, and taken in carts to their graves."

Betsy and John were terrified for their children, especially their babies, Rachel, who had been born in February 1789, and ten-month-old Jane. Although Betsy, John, and their girls stayed well, yellow fever hit the Griscom family hard. Betsy's mother, father, and oldest sister, Deborah, died. Only the coming of cold weather and frost put an end to the epidemic.

Sarah Donaldson's orphaned daughter, Sarah Donaldson II, had been living with her Aunt Deborah. When Deborah died, Betsy welcomed fourteen-year-old Sarah into the Claypoole family. John was good-natured about adding another young woman to a household that included Betsy, Eliza, Clarissa, Susan, Rachel, and Jane. With six girls, as well as the shop, the Claypoole house was full to overflowing. Betsy and John decided to move again. This time they leased a house at 72 Front Street between Chestnut and Walnut.

The Claypooles' move to larger quarters came just in time. Their shop had suddenly become busier than ever with flag orders. In 1795, the design of the American flag was changed for the first time. After two new states, Vermont and Kentucky, were admitted to the Union, Congress passed a flag act. The new flag would have fifteen stars and fifteen stripes. Because Congress still hadn't directed how the stars should be placed, flag makers used their imaginations. A favorite design arranged the fifteen stars into a single five-pointed star.

The Claypooles' larger house came in handy in more ways than one. The year that the flag design was changed was the same year that Betsy gave birth to her seventh daughter. Harriet was born on December 20, 1795. Because Betsy, at age forty-three, had no plans for more children, she, and the rest of the family, took special pleasure in baby Harriet. But in September 1796 their joy was cut short. Nine-month-old Harriet died.

So many deaths in so short a time. Betsy had lost her oldest daughter, and now her youngest was gone. Although Betsy and John were grief-stricken, they still had six young women to raise and a shop to run. Despite their sorrow, they carried on.

The year after Harriet's death, Betsy welcomed another niece into the family, her sister Sarah's oldest daughter. Twenty-two-year-old Margaret Donaldson Boggs's husband and son had died, and she was alone and adrift. Betsy knew only too well what it was like to lose a husband and a child, and she welcomed Margaret warmly.

All of Betsy's nieces and nephews and even her distant cousin, John Griscom, who arrived in Philadelphia to teach school, turned to Betsy for love, understanding, and advice. She made them feel wanted *and* useful. When her daughters and nieces were old enough, she put them to work in the shop.

Great Aunt Sarah had taught Betsy everything she knew. Betsy, in turn, taught her daughters and nieces everything that she knew. Great Aunt Sarah had been the matriarch of the Griscom family during Betsy's growing-up years. Now Betsy had become the matriarch of her family. Loving, generous, and steady in a crisis, Betsy's spirit drew everyone to her.

CHAPTER 24

With the Claypoole shop well staffed by both family and outside help, John grew restless. He was ready for a new challenge. When he was offered a government job at the United States Custom House in Philadelphia, he accepted. Once again Betsy took full charge of the business.

In the years that followed, John did well at the Custom House, and his salary paid for pleasant extras. The shop flourished. Betsy and John's girls grew into fine young women. The family continued to worship at the Free Quaker Meeting, which was growing and prospering.

On January 1, 1800, Betsy turned forty-eight. Her birthday marked the beginning of a new century, rich with possibilities for the future. Betsy's favorite hero,

George Washington, just missed greeting the new century. He had died on December 14, 1799. Betsy had felt a special connection with George Washington ever since that long-ago day when he had come to her shop.

The new century brought changes to Philadelphia. In November 1800, Washington, D.C., became the nation's new capital. The president, Congress, the Supreme Court, and most U.S. government offices left Philadelphia. City traffic had often been snarled, and the noise had sometimes been deafening. Nevertheless, Betsy missed the pomp and ceremony.

Life for the Claypooles was changing, too. The serious wounds that John had suffered at Germantown and his years in Old Mill Prison had taken their toll. His health began to fail. Before long, he could no longer work, and he resigned his Custom House job.

As usual, Betsy rose to the crisis. She had been the family's sole wage earner before, and she could do it again. Besides, this time she had plenty of family to help her.

But John's health didn't improve and he continued to grow weaker. Betsy left more and more of the shop business to others as she cared for her husband. She nursed him through his sickly days and cheered him up when he was depressed. Through it all, Betsy refused to let the house become a gloomy hospital. As the girls began to marry and have children of their own, the Claypooles celebrated many happy times.

Then, on June 18, 1812, war was again declared against Great Britain. During the War of 1812, Betsy sold flags to shipping firms, merchants, and military organizations. Stephen Girard, a wealthy Philadelphian whose ships sailed all over the world, was one of Betsy's steady customers. Even though Betsy was still listed in the Philadelphia directory as an upholsterer, for the next few years, her shop turned out more flags than anything else.

Betsy's daughter Clarissa and her niece Margaret Boggs were especially helpful during the war. The other girls had moved away with their husbands, and Betsy needed all the help she could get. John's condition had worsened. Soon after the war ended, he suffered a stroke. On August 3, 1817, John Claypoole died just days before his sixty-fifth birthday.

John's death came as no surprise to Betsy. He had been sick for a long time. But she and John had been married for thirty-four years, and she was devastated.

Betsy was sixty-five herself now and she was tired from the years of nursing her husband. Everyone in the family was urging her to take time to enjoy her grandchildren. Perhaps she should retire.

CHAPTER 25

In the end, Betsy decided that retirement wasn't for her. After losing three husbands and two children, she had learned that she was happiest when she was working. She stayed on and managed the business for another ten years.

Although Betsy was energetic and strong and her mind was as clear as ever, her family kept at her to retire. Finally, at the age of seventy-five, she turned the business over to her daughter Clarissa and her niece Margaret Boggs.

Betsy may have retired in 1827, but for years the Philadelphia City Directory listed her as "Elizabeth Claypoole, upholsterer." And Betsy always wore her scissors and silver-ringed needle ball on her chatelaine as a proud mark of her trade. She even added something new. In her pocket, she carried a small silver snuff box that she took out from time to time for a pinch of snuff.

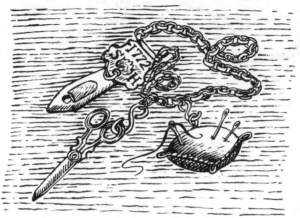

Betsy's daughters all wanted her to live with them. Her daughter Susan won out. Susan and her husband, Abel Satterthwaite, welcomed Betsy into their home in Abington, just north of Philadelphia.

During summer family get-togethers, Betsy gathered her granddaughters around her and taught them the simple needlework and quilting stitches that Great Aunt Sarah had once taught her. And her standards of excellence were as high as ever. The girls adored their grandmother and worked hard to win her approval.

Like Great Aunt Sarah, Betsy held her grandchildren spellbound with tales of being a young woman in Philadelphia. Of all the stories, the children's favorite was how George Washington had come to her little shop on Arch Street. She told them, too, about those exciting times when the Declaration of Independence and the Constitution had been drawn up in the State House, which the grandchildren knew as Independence Hall. No doubt she taught them the jingle that had once helped her to remember the names of Philadelphia's streets.

High, Mulberry, Sassafrass, Vine,
Chestnut, Walnut, Spruce, and Pine.

For some time, Betsy was able to travel the twelve miles back and forth to Philadelphia from her daughter's Abington home. One family member would put her on the stage coach, and another would pick her up in Philadelphia. While she was in the city, she faithfully attended the Free Quaker Meetings.

And then Betsy's eyesight began to fail. She could no longer sew and was able to read only in bright sunlight. When she reached the age of eighty, she had to admit that the trip in and out of the city was too much for her. In 1833, she moved back to Philadelphia to live with her daughter and son-in-law, Jane and Caleb Canby.

Betsy continued to attend Free Quaker Meetings. Because none of her daughters had memories of being disowned as she had, they had drifted away from the Society of Free Quakers and joined traditional Quaker Meetings. The other members had drifted away, too. By 1834, Betsy and the grandson of the original founder of the Free Quakers were the only ones left. For weeks, Betsy and John Wetherill sat silently in the ministers' gallery facing the empty benches.

"Widow Claypoole, there are but two of us remaining," John Wetherill was reported to have said. "It is not right that thee and I should continue to meet here alone."

Reluctantly, Betsy agreed. The end of the Society of Free Quakers was the end of a source of great comfort and strength in her life. It was a sad moment when John Wetherill locked the door for the last time with the large, old-fashioned key and the two of them went their separate ways.

Although Betsy became blind in her last days and seldom left the house, she was surrounded by love. As her health continued to fail, she was soon confined to bed. At eighty-four, Betsy had seen enough of death to have no fear of it. Her faith and her family sustained her, and she died peacefully on January 30, 1836.

Her grandson William Canby recalled that night. "For three days we went on tip-toe about the house and in and out of the little room by the back parlor where the apparently lifeless form of Grandmother lay upon her bed. On the third [day], after dinner, we all went in to see her die; and so gently, so like her life, that we could not see that she was not still sleeping."

Elizabeth Griscom Ross Ashburn Claypoole was buried beside John Claypoole in the Free Quaker Burial Grounds.

Betsy had been born on a special date, the first day of the first month of the first year in the new calendar. She had witnessed the birth of a new nation and made the first flag of that nation. Betsy had earned more than a place in the heart of her family. She had earned a lasting place in the heart of America.

AUTHOR'S NOTE

No written records exist to prove that Betsy Ross sewed the first Stars and Stripes flag. However, it is known that George Washington was in Philadelphia in late May and early June 1776. It is also known that he was concerned with the design of a national flag during that time.

Betsy's daughter Clarissa Claypoole Wilson and Betsy's niece Margaret Boggs lived and worked with Betsy for many years. Both women signed witnessed and notarized affidavits stating that Betsy had told them that George Washington, Robert Morris, and George Ross had come to her Arch Street shop in 1776 to commission a flag.

Betsy's daughter Rachel Claypoole Fletcher, two

granddaughters and two grandnieces also signed witnessed and notarized affidavits confirming that Betsy had told them about her meeting with George Washington and his committee in 1776. Betsy, her daughters, her niece, her granddaughters, and grandnieces were devout Quakers. As such, they were women of unquestionable honesty.

In 1925, a descendant of Samuel Wetherill, the founder of the Society of Free Quakers, opened a long-sealed safe, which contained a paper pattern for a five-pointed star. Betsy's daughter Clarissa, who carried on her mother's business until 1857, had signed the paper pattern. The fact that it was signed and put away for safekeeping indicates its significance to the family, as well as the possibility that it was Betsy's original star pattern.

Although there are those who question that Betsy Ross made the first national flag, none of them has been able to produce any conclusive evidence to the contrary. For the commissioning of the flag by George Washington and his committee in 1776, I have relied on three books: *Betsy Ross: The Griscom Legacy* by Dr. William D. Timmins and Robert W. Yarrington, Jr., and Robert Morris's *The Truth About the American Flag* and *The Truth About the Betsy Ross Story.*

BIBLIOGRAPHY

Bacon, Margaret Hope. *The Quiet Rebels.* Philadelphia: New Society, 1985.

Betsy Ross House Archives. *Pennsylvania Gazette,* articles 1766–83; files; notebooks; reports; research papers. Philadelphia.

Boorstein, Daniel J. *The Americans: The Colonial Experience.* New York: Random House, 1958.

Bridenbaugh, Carl, and Jessica Bridenbaugh. *Rebels and Gentlemen: Philadelphia in the Age of Franklin.* New York: Reynal & Hitchcock, 1942.

Brinton, Howard H. *Guide to Quaker Practice.* Wallingford, Pa.: Pendle Hill, 1993.

Cooke, Edward S., Jr. *Upholstery in America and Europe from the Seventeenth Century to World War I.* New York: W. W. Norton & Co., 1987.

Crane, Elaine Forman, ed. *The Diary of Elizabeth Drinker.* Boston: Northeastern University Press, 1994.

Duane, William, ed. *Extracts from the Diary of Christopher Marshall, 1774–1781.* New York: New York Times & Arno Press, 1969.

Earle, Alice Morse. *Home Life in Colonial Days.* New York: Macmillan, 1898.

Elgin, Kathleen. *The Quakers: The Religious Society of Friends.* New York: David McKay, 1968.

Jackson, John W. *With the British Army in Philadelphia, 1777–1778.* San Rafael, Calif.: Presidio Press, 1979.

Jenkins, Charles Francis. "John Claypoole's Memorandum Book." *Pennsylvania Magazine of History and Biography,* vol. 16.

Morris, Richard B. *Independence.* Washington, D.C.: Government Printing Office, 1982.

Morris, Robert. *The Truth About the American Flag.* Beach Haven, N.J.: Wynnehaven, 1978.

————. *The Truth About the Betsy Ross Story.* Beach Haven, N.J.: Wynnehaven, 1982.

Parry, Edwin S. *Betsy Ross, Quaker Rebel.* Philadelphia: John C. Winston, 1930.

Quaife, Milo, Melvin J. Weig, and Roy E. Appleman. *The History of the United States Flag.* New York: Harper, 1961.

Riley, Edward M. *The Story of Independence Hall.* Gettysburg, Pa.: Thomas, 1980.

Timmins, William D., and Robert W. Yarrington, Jr. *Betsy Ross: The Griscom Legacy.* Woodstown, N.J.: The

Salem County Cultural and Heritage Commission, 1983.

Weigley, Russell F., ed. *Philadelphia: A 300-Year History.* New York: W. W. Norton, 1982.

Wilbur, C. Keith. *Pirates and Patriots of the Revolution.* Old Saybrook, Conn.: Globe Pequot Press, 1984.

Wolf, Edwin, II. *Philadelphia: Portrait of an American City.* Harrisburg, Pa.: Stackpole Books, 1975.